True You

A Self-Discovery Journal for the
Curious Heart

Jillian Bolanz

True You
A Self-Discovery Journal for the Curious Heart

Editor: Sally Leger

Acknowledgements for Production Support:
Michael Bolanz
Sally Leger
Missy Reber
Lynn Montgomery
Rachel Pelletier
Amber Lilyestrom's Mastermind Soul Sisters

ISBN: 9781973275138

For more, visit **www.jillianbolanz.com**

or email **jillian@jillianbolanz.com**

or join the Empowered Love Notes email list **www.jillianbolanz.com/empower**

Connect with Jillian on social media:
Facebook : www.facebook.com/JillianBolanz
Instagram: @jillianbolanz
LinkedIn: Jillian Bolanz
Podcast: Morning Sunshine with Jillian Bolanz

For Michael, Cameron, and Andrew –

Thank you for your unending support and love. You are the reasons I care to always seek to discover the True Me... It allows for me to be the very best me for you. And you, my loves, deserve the very best!

I love you so much!

Introduction – You're Ready!

Hey there, you incredibly FABULOUS human! Welcome to True You: Self-Discovery Journal for the Introspective Beginner! I am so psyched to have you here and I know that you are holding this beautiful book for two reasons:

1. You want to know yourself better. Things are good... but you know there is so much more to you and you are ready to maximize on this amazing life and human experience!

2. You want to learn how to incorporate journaling in your life. Journaling intrigues you, but it also makes you feel a little uncomfortable and you can't get past the dreamy "Dear Diary" phrase that you leaned on heavily during middle school days. You want to move beyond that so that you can effectively use this amazing exercise!

My friend, you have come to the right place. This is the journal for you! I have 50 days' worth of prompts and guidance coming your way! Before we dive into putting your pen to the page, I am going to teach you all that I have discovered about journaling as I started leaning into it. I'm going to speak to you in the way that I speak to myself, my family, and my friends- because I want you to FEEL my energy. My hope is that you will learn the lessons, read my words, and trust my guidance so that I can condense the timeline of your self-discovery. The way I will present journaling and using that as a tool for self-discovery to you is how I would have loved it to be presented to me – like your best friend getting to the point of what you have to do but then loving you through the process!

So, here we go!

Quick Connection Story

For me there came a point where it was very clear that I no longer wanted to be, do, or think the way I always had. There was a stirring within me that told me I was meant for more – to feel deeper, to become better aligned, to discontinue floating through life and checking off boxes. It was time to start living more purposefully and in alignment with my passions and what my soul was put on earth to do.

This meant that I would have to make some changes to my external world and it became very clear that to do that (because I had no idea what that meant or looked like) I needed to FINALLY gain clarity on my internal world.

No longer did I want to do things just because that was the prescription I had given myself. I wanted to KNOW myself. I wanted to be able to trust myself. I wanted to be able to answer the whisperings of my heart and I intuitively knew that to do this, I needed to spend more time understanding WHO I really was.

People say things like "Oh just go out and find your passion" or "Listen to your heart" or "Trust your instincts"… but seriously, what does all that even MEAN?!

It sounds great, but quite honestly, listening to our internal, wisest voice - the dialogue that derives from our soul - is a lot like listening to a foreign language. Unless we spend time LEARNING that language – listening to it, understanding it, and speaking it - we will stand there blankly (probably feeling frustrated) as we try to surmise the directions that are coming at us through words, feelings, and other prompts that we just don't understand.

So, how do we start learning the internal language of our True-Self?

Well, if you are holding this amazing journal in your hands, I BET you are intuitive enough to know that I am going to tell you that JOURNALING is the way to learn the internal language of our TRUE SELF!

For me, journaling is the most profound way to take what is going on within me and allowing for it to come out. I can become connected to what I feel through my human senses of sight (seeing the words on the page) and touch (feeling the pen pour my heart's' truth physically onto the page). This is so important because when you pour the words of your inner truth onto a page it allows for you to physically connect with and mentally and emotionally witness the energy within you.

Now, you picked up this journal for SOME reason… you are obviously feeling even the tiniest pull to learning more about it, but let's quickly deal with some thoughts that may have kept you from journaling in the past…

YOUR THOUGHT: "I don't like writing and have never been a writer."
MY EMPOWERING RESPONSE: Honestly, you've never made it a priority and now you GET to do so. You GET to learn a new skill and, in the process, you GET to know yourself better. Go you!

YOUR THOUGHT: "I don't have time to sit down and write."
MY EMPOWERING RESPONSE: I'll give you a tool that will help you to reframe "time" with journaling later, but the fact is, you do have the time. We all have the same 24 hours in a day. You just have never chosen to dedicate your time toward journaling. And that's okay! But if you want to feel a change in how you know yourself, you need to make a change in how you go about self-discovery. And for some, that simply means beginning SOMETHING new. That was me, and journaling was it!

When you journal, a few things happen:

1. When you allow the pen to flow, you get through the surface "stuff" and just write, you WILL tap into deeper places within you that will allow for thoughts, feelings, experiences, and emotions to be discovered.

   YOUR THOUGHT: "Yeah right… that doesn't really happen."
   MY EMPOWERING RESPONSE: Yes it does, I promise it does. And I can wholeheartedly say that because I didn't believe it either, until I got to the point in my journaling journey where I would look down and say "where the flipping heck did THAT thought/ emotion/ buried experience/ idea/ etc. come from?"

   YOUR THOUGHT: "I don't know if I really WANT to uncover some of the things I've got buried deep inside."
   MY EMPOWERING RESPONSE: I honor you so much for acknowledging this fear, but again, yes you do. You do because you are determined to live a more fulfilled life and when you do the deep digging, you get to find the blocks that have been keeping you stuck and release them. You also get to discover the true power you have within you that has been covered up for so long.

   *Note… I know where your mind went and no, journaling is not all about uncovering painful, fear-based, uncomfortable STUFF. In fact, the way that I journal and will teach you to journal will always start with gratitude and be abundantly about discovering JOY… but it is through journaling that you DO get to look at the fear-based thoughts that have kept you STUCK so that you can move through them.

Getting to know both what brings you joy and what makes you super uncomfortable- is so helpful (and so necessary) and will provide you with the opportunity to continue to grow in love with YOU.

As you gain clarity on the things that bring you JOY, you will know that you want to do more of those things and you GET to make them a priority. As you gain clarity on the things that cause you pain you GET to witness and release them so that they no longer plague you, which of course, makes space for joy to come in.

No matter what your journaling reveals- love or fear- it's a win/win because it is going to help you align with doing more of the things that make you feel good and less of the things that make you feel uncomfortable, less than, or scared!

I know that you may have been hesitant to journaling in the past because you've been scared of discovering and rediscovering the wounds within you... don't be. You are going to uncover a lot of GOOD (that you would never have found because you assumed you would only find tough stuff) and remember to ask yourself this: what's scarier? Finding a fear and getting to detoxify yourself

of it as you step into your brilliance or holding on to it and walking around with that fear holding the true you captive inside simply because you refused to look at it?

2. For my strategy seekers, my logistics lovers, my "but HOW will this happen?!" wonderers, my "would someone please just give me the rules, directions, and roadmap to follow" demanders –first of all, I feel you, I am you.

   Second: THERE YOU GO! You just wrote it down in your journal. **The energetically sound "rule book" of your soul just printed itself out on the page in front of you.** Because the truth of who we are, what we are meant to do, what we feel most connected to, has been there all along. We all know what to do. We just have too much crap mucking up our internal GPS, causing our directions to get lost in translation. **When we journal we are literally putting on paper the roadmap of our soul.**

3. By default, you not only allow yourself the opportunity to gain clarity on who you truly are, **but you also create physical and energetic space around you that proclaims to the world that you are making yourself a priority**. Because you will likely journal during a quiet time of the day you will have more opportunity to reflect upon the miracles that surround you. You are probably laughing at the concept of "quiet time of the day" ... but we're going to find it for you. That time is there and I'm going to teach you how to it a priority. You'll quickly see how important it is to your True You!

4. **Your relationships will be more fulfilled.** You may not realize it now, but it is likely that you expect others to fix you and to fill a void that was created through your own insecurities. It is likely that you have been waiting for someone to save you and tell you what to do. This causes your relationships to be based on dependency rather than co-creation. (Don't worry- they are likely doing that to you too... you should probably recommend to them that they get this journal as well...) Since you will be allowing for yourself to "go there" with working through struggles and uncovering strengths, you won't have to depend on a spouse, child, sibling, parent, co-worker, or friend to do it for you... causing a heck of a lot LESS pressure for that person. This will open the opportunity for those relationships to become more deeply connected through LOVE rather than rooted in fear and expectation.

5. **You will learn to surrender, trust, ask for guidance, and feel more connected, spiritually, to a higher power than you ever have before.** Yep, I'm going there. I'm not going to tell you what or who to "believe in" when it comes to Spirit. But I am going to tell you that when you allow for yourself to get really real with what you FEEL connected to, and you allow for yourself to acknowledge that there is a higher power that is right there, asking for you to co-create life along with it, magic happens.

You are not in this alone.

Phew… did you just breathe a sigh of relief? It is not just YOU who has to "figure this out". You are held and supported and if you are open and ready to receive it, you are being guided in a way that is congruent with what your soul WANTS.

Call it God, the Universe, Divine Spirit, Energy… seriously call it whatever you want… **I call it Love.** I call the energetic force that I can tap into, be guided by, and align with Love. And it is through journaling that I get to connect, not just to the truth that my heart calls to, but to the internal knowledge that I am being held as I flow through this self-discovery process.

When I started my self-discovery journey at the beginning of 2017, it was based on the fact that I had no idea what I believed in/ aligned with/ felt connected to on a spiritual level. I knew the "rules" of religion (and I will add, I am grateful for the education I have received through religious teachings) but I had a deep yearning to go beyond the rules and tap into connection with the divine LOVE that I intuitively believe God is. Journaling helped me to strip away the rules, release the teachings, and deeply connect with what I believe to be true: that God is Love, and the True Me is Love, and when that LOVE leads the way, my life will reflect my truth.

Now, I'm not encouraging you to discount religious teachings. What I am encouraging you to do though is ask the questions that you have burning within you and go deep within to answer them. I'm asking you to think differently… feel differently. I'm asking that you go into this whole new process and practice with an air of OPENNESS. You want to get to know yourself better and deeper? Being open to the fact that you don't have to do it alone (like you have been doing up to this point) and in fact, there is a divine power that is bigger than you. Be open to allowing yourself to be supported. Be open; allow however you define LOVE to present itself by way of connecting with the True You.

6. **You will fall in love with you.** You will get to know who you really are. You will connect with your creativity, inspiration, and truth. And THAT, right there, is everything!

But How?!

So, these things all rock, right?! It's super exciting to gain clarity for yourself, improve your relationships, actually OWN some quiet time, connect with whatever you define as Love and Spirit... but HOW?

Okay, here's what I know to be true:

You have heard people talk about journaling. You have received the "you should totally journal on that and see what comes up" advice from people. You KNOW that successful people (aptly dubbed by YOUR definition and perception of success) that you admire spend time journaling. So, you know that there MUST be something to it, right? I mean, logically all these people in the world wouldn't talk about journaling if it wasn't helpful. There actually wouldn't even be journals like this one, or any pretty notebook you find at your local book store, if the physical product wasn't being used to serve people. So rationally, if there are people who do it and the physical product is there, it is safe to surmise that the practice makes SENSE to do.

But you have no idea where to start!

And truthfully, you don't know if it's WORTH starting. Not only do you not know if you will "stick with it" but, deep down, you don't want to be disappointed. You don't want to feel like it's not helping. You don't want to feel as though it's not doing for you what it has done for others. You don't know if it will "live up" to the hype. You don't know if you will sabotage yourself. You don't know if you WANT to. Don't don't don't. Lack lack lack.

And it's okay... because you DO know one thing: You are READY to dig in and figure out who you TRULY are. And if you trust that journaling will be the portal for that self-discovery that you yearn for (and deserve) ... you will do it anyway.

Forget all the reasons why you haven't tried journaling. Forget all the reasons why you may not always feel like journaling. Remember WHY you care to learn about it NOW. You are ready to know your True Self and no longer are you going to let logistical excuses of "I don't know how to journal" stand in your way!

You've got this. You're empowered. You're ready.

What's coming!

On the following pages, I will present to you some different ideas on how to actively journal. Do what feels best. That is the one rule for all of this... do what you FEEL most connected to. Do what feels easiest/ lightest/ most aligned. **Journal in the way that brings you JOY.**

We are also going to talk about how to structure your journaling. I know that when I first started journaling, the first question I asked was: "So what are the rules to journaling?" Some people like to free flow with their words – grab a book and a pen and let it all pour out. I needed to follow a little more of a guideline at first because, truthfully, sitting there in the silence with my thoughts was uncomfortable and I found that without a relative plan and prompts, my thoughts got jumbled in my head. So, we are going to talk about the "how-to's" of structuring your daily journaling.

Once we know the "how-to's" we dive into the good stuff. Once you are armed and comfortable with the outline of journaling, and the physical act is no longer a barrier, it is time to unlock and connect with your True Self within.

I am going to help you start peeling back the onion layers within and helping you along your self-discovery process. I'm going to ask prompting questions and teach mini-lessons for you to reflect upon and respond to. I will also provide you with affirmations to expound upon in your own words. This will begin the transformative process of stepping into the person you truly are in a way that is eye opening, healing, and illuminating.

I also encourage you to add an extra layer of accountability and connection by subscribing to my Podcast on iTunes called "Morning Sunshine with Jillian Bolanz" for daily inspiration and empowered conversations. On this podcast I have 5 minute(ish) conversations to kick start your gratitude, affirmations, and present you with a "morning pep talk". I encourage my listeners to grab their journals and use my verbal prompts as invitations to soul search and get whatever comes up onto the page!

The "Rules" of Journaling

First, there are no hard and fast rules that apply to everyone. Journaling is a very personal and private matter and you GET to do it in the way that feels best for you. That being said, here are some thoughts about how you can get started with the concept of journaling:

1. **Grab a journal and a pen.** You've already got this amazing beauty right here- this is for you. THIS is your journal. But I will add, if I see a journal or notebook that sparks something within me (maybe it's pretty, maybe it's sturdy, maybe the pages just seem super inviting) I will get it for myself because I always want to feel super connected to the physical product I am pouring my soul into. So, utilize this True You Self-Discovery Journal, get 100 of them as long as it feels right, and just be open to always having a vessel with you into which you can pour your heart.

    Also, the pen is key. I have about 15 of the same type of pen in every nook and cranny of my LIFE: my desk, my kitchen, my purse, my travel bags, my cars, etc. I LOVE the way that pen writes and again, if it FEELS good, I am much more likely to allow for my thoughts to pour through it.

    Side note- my entire family is well aware of the fact that those particular pens are "Mumma's pens" and may appear to be there for anyone's use but they are strategically placed for my writing purposes… aka, back of my pens, boys!

2. **Decide if you want to journal for X number of pages or X amount of time.** This may seem like a silly distinction, but it meant everything to me. I am a highly efficient person and I tend to live by the "no moment wasted" mentality. For some reason, the thought of "sit down and journal for 10 minutes" didn't feel great because it restricted me in one sense (what if I'm on a roll and really want to get these feelings on to the page but I only "gave" myself 10 minutes to bust it out?) and provided me with too much wiggle room on the other end (what if I feel stressed about other things that require my time and can't come up with anything to write about and I end up sitting there for 10 minutes doing nothing when I could have been doing something else?).

    So, I reframed the experience and instead of leaving it up to the devices of something I feel more negatively charged around (time), I decided to encourage myself to fill three pages. No matter what, I was going to fill three pages. It didn't matter how fast or slow the process took… it didn't matter how cohesive the thoughts were… as long as I was getting words on to three pages I knew I was making progress in a way that felt more aligned with the True Me.

    In this journal, I have provided three pages per day for each of the 50 days' worth of gratitude reflection opportunities and prompts!

3. **Determine WHEN you are going to journal.** Pick a time of day and schedule it. Enter "journaling time" right into your calendar. Tell your family, tell your boss, tell your mailman, tell YOURSELF and do it. The time of day is up to you but I will say that it is preferable that you pick a time where your environment is able to be quiet and still. A time where you feel calm and can tap into your joy. The stillness around you will allow for you to be still within and that is how you start cracking your heart wide open to let your inner light shine.

   I know you're busy. We all are. But this important because YOU are important. Some quick thoughts on how to sneak in some journaling time may include: wake up 10 minutes earlier, spend your lunch break journaling, recognize how often you are scrolling through Instagram and allow for that to be the trigger for snagging your journal instead, grab your journal and commit to spending time with it before you turn on the television at night, etc. There are so many ways to fit it in. You have time; now you GET to make it! Schedule it in!

4. **Pick the place based on how you are feeling THAT day.** Some people will tell you to journal in the same location every single day- to establish a sanctuary and go to that one spot that you feel safe, supported, and most open every single time. I think that is GREAT advice- if that's what you want to do each and every day. For me, I choose the location of journaling based on an intuitive feeling I have within. Some days I want to journal at my desk in my office with the head light off and the salt lamp lit. Some days I want to journal on our comfy, over stuffed couch in the basement. Some days I want to physically be closer to my family (who are usually sleeping while I journal) so I will choose to sit in the living room. Some days I want to journal outside.

   I sit where I feel most connected on that day and I trust that if I wanted to be in that space, then that is exactly where I feel most supported. If that happens to be the same place for you every day- rock on, friend. Own it! For me, it's not, and that's okay!

5. **My friend... commit to yourself that you are going to do this.** Remind yourself that the TRUE YOU is worth knowing, worth discovering, worth uncovering. Logistically, this is important; but energetically, this is everything. I encourage you to complete the following... consider this your first assignment in journaling...

   I, _____, commit to discovering my True Self. I commit to doing this through the art and practice of journaling. I commit to myself that I will show up for myself and the life I am meant to create by, every single day, allowing for the love that is within me to shine through. I am EXCITED to uncover who I truly am by way of journaling!

In this journal, not only will I be giving you different prompts, questions to answer, affirmations to reflect upon and write about, but I will be introducing you to different ways to write it out. Sometimes I will encourage you to let the thoughts "free flow" from your pen onto the page. Sometimes I will encourage you to write a letter - perhaps to yourself or to someone else. Other times we will focus on the energy blocks you are feeling. We will write about past, present, and future experiences. We will write about joy often. We will write about grief, and how to move through and past it. On occasion, we will write about forgiveness. No matter what though, I want you to enjoy the experience of learning HOW TO journal and allowing for that to be the catalyst that will help you unlock your True Self!

And with all that being said...
Let's get journaling!

Day 1

Gratitude: What are you grateful for?!

Prompt: Who are you? I know that the point of this journal is for you to figure out who you are - the TRUE YOU at your core. I would love to give you the opportunity now to start to step into it. It will be amazing to see the transformation of how you will answer this question from the first day to the final day in this journal. So go there. Start writing it out. You may want to make a bulleted list or simply let your pen flow. Start with who you are with surface level stuff, and then continue to go deeper. When you think you are done, don't stop... keep going... there is more to you than will immediately come to your mind. Allow for the True You voice to come through as you write... open your heart, listen to what it whispers, and go for it!

Day 2

Gratitude: What makes your heart soar with happiness?!

Prompt: How can you love yourself more? This is the ultimate question I want you to answer. I want you to release the burden you have put onto others to "fix you" and understand right here and now that it is no one else's job to make you feel whole besides YOU. To do that you must learn how to love yourself more without expectation and/or ties to the outside world. Here are some more questions that can help you navigate this very complex question: How have you been unkind to yourself? Where have you been holding yourself back from showing yourself appreciation? Who have you depended on to love you so that you can coast by without loving yourself? Who have you placed external blame on for why you are unable to love yourself: "This person makes me feel _____", "This person doesn't allow for me to _____"? It's time to call BS on blaming the world and own up to the fact that no matter what is going on outside of you, it is up to YOU to love what is right there within you!

_____

_____

_____

_____

_____

_____

_____

_____

Day 3

Gratitude: What are you pumped up about today?!

Prompt: Fear. Fear is the opposite of love. In this process of learning who we are and learning how to love our True Self, it's so important that we recognize how fearful we are of feelings, situations, people, perceptions, things, etc. And here is the thing… fear will keep popping up. Even if we think we have dealt with something, those nasty feelings that keep us small, hold us back, and block us from our truth (which is love) will try to weasel their way back in. So, today we are going to focus on reframing fears and creating loving truths instead.

I would like for you to draw a line down the center of the pages for this section. Please write out FEARS over the column on the left side and TRUTH over the column on the right side. Write out each fear you can think of in the FEARS column (we are talking everything from fear of what others think, to fear of not being lovable, to fear of failure, to fear of success… ANYTHING) and in the TRUTH column, I'd love for you to flip that fear statement on its head. Learn how to see your fears differently. List your fears, look at them objectively and see for yourself how they don't have to be your truth! When you write the opposite of your fear on the right side, you assert to yourself that your fears are based on limiting beliefs and you don't have to own them anymore.

(Example: Fear- I am fearful of starting my own business because I am too shy. Opportunity Thought- Success in business does not only come to one personality type, this fear is not true! Truth- I am brave and capable of building an extremely successful business.)

Day 4

Gratitude: What makes you want to have your own, personal dance party?

Prompt: "I choose to release my fears." How's THAT for an affirmation? How did you like the exercise we did yesterday? It's really nice to have the opportunity to witness the truth that lives on the other side of your fear! However, the work isn't done yet. We know that our fears are lies that we have been telling ourselves and although we have seen the other side, where love lives, we still need to release what has been holding us back. Today, I'd like for you to write the words "I choose to release my fears" at the top of the page and write yourself a letter. I'd like for you to go back and review your fears from yesterday and write to yourself, giving yourself permission to witness all that you have been fearful of (without judgement), and absolve yourself from those thoughts and worries. It's time to release those fears. It's time to give yourself permission to move past them. Write yourself a letter explaining how and why you choose to release your fears. Have fun - this is powerful and super healing. Enjoy this rejuvenation process as you let love replace your fears.

Day 5

Gratitude: Because acknowledging what you are grateful for honors the work of your past self... what you have now is something you once wanted... be grateful for all that you have provided yourself with!

Prompt: Ask for what you need. So often we walk around with hopes and desires and we expect the world to simply know what it is we want. Whether it is from other people or from God, it is important to ask for what you need. Giving yourself, others, and the Universe specific insight into what you truly need is the greatest gift you can give. This gets the guess work, fuzziness, and miscommunication out of the way! When what you need is clear, then it can be delivered to you. So, what is it that you truly need? What is it your heart longs for? And from whom do you need it? Get specific- clarity will allow for miracles to unfold.

Day 6

Gratitude: Oh HAPPY day! How are you choosing joy today?

Prompt: In what ways do you need to forgive? How have you allowed disappointment to keep you stuck? (This includes disappointment in yourself, others, experiences, life...) Holding on to things that feel heavy (emotionally, mentally, spiritually, and physically) not only doesn't serve you, but it keeps you from being able to step into your brilliance. And the way out of that, to releasing these things is through forgiveness! Free flow. Tap into the True You and allow the truth of forgiveness to set you free!

_____

_____

_____

_____

_____

_____

_____

_____

_____

_____

_____

_____

_____

Day 7

Gratitude: What have you experienced, felt, witnessed, chosen, etc. over the past week that you are so flippin' grateful for?

Prompt: Celebrate. What do you need to celebrate right now? We spend so much time looking forward – working toward goals, checking boxes, and DOING – that we forget to look back and acknowledge what we've DONE! (Ahem... like completing a weeks' worth of journaling for, possibly, the first time ever...). Today, celebrate YOU. Celebrate the way you feel. Celebrate the curveballs that have been thrown your way. Celebrate you range of feelings you are able to experience. Celebrate and be grateful! Spend some time here in celebration mode. What are you celebrating today?

_____

_____

_____

_____

_____

_____

_____

_____

_____

_____

_____

Day 8

Gratitude: Oh, Thank you, Universe for _____!

Prompt: Be okay with being a work in progress. You are never going to have it all figured out. None of us have ever done THIS life before... we are all doing, growing, learning, and living the best way we can. Today just let the pen flow... what's been on your heart? What feels heavy right now? Get it out and allow for the answer to bubble to the surface.

_____

_____

_____

_____

_____

_____

_____

_____

_____

_____

_____

_____

_____

Day 9

Gratitude: It's right there within you, what are you grateful for?

Prompt: Have you been thrown a "what the HELL" yet? I know when I first started uncovering fears and upleveling myself, I got thrown a couple serious blows from outside sources that had me saying, "What the HELL?! I'm working on bettering myself... why do I feel like there are energies trying to knock me down?!" LOVE those moments... they are opportunities for GROWTH and for you to assert the fact that you are FINALLY going there... you are FINALLY not going to give up on yourself! Write a letter to your present self today. Reassure yourself that you are exactly where you are meant to be. Acknowledge that you have tilled up some "stuff" and that you have been thrown some curveballs, and remind yourself how resilient you are. TALK to yourself (through your writing) about how uncomfortable some of this has been, cheer yourself on, and remind yourself that you are going to do it anyway. Remember to sign it with LOVE.

_____

_____

_____

_____

_____

_____

_____

_____

_____

Day 10

Gratitude: So many good things are swirling around you, which of these things are making you feel elated?

Prompt: Here is another affirmation for you today... write this one down and reflect upon it. "Let go and flow!" In what areas of your life are you still gripping the steering wheel so hard that your knuckles are turning white? Where do you need to surrender and let God drive? As you journal today, list out the areas that you have been uneasy about relinquishing your human control and then ask yourself, "How would I feel if I were supported in this?" Sit with the feeling of flow that comes when you realize that the most complex areas in our life (that we feel we must force our ways through) actually provide us with the greatest opportunity to release and flow with the inspired direction of energy sources around us.

_____

_____

_____

_____

_____

_____

_____

_____

_____

_____

_____

Gratitude: Shout it out – what are you grateful for?

Prompt: Yesterday we talked about choosing flow over force. Some things may have been easy for you to release once it was brought to your attention. With other things you may feel like you can't simply release without making a bigger decision. When this is the case, our intuition is our greatest teacher and innately knows the answer- we must be willing to get still and listen to it. Today, write down that one thing that you just keep battling back and forth. Perhaps you feel like you've made a decision, but it keeps resurfacing as unfinished. If you have "made a decision" but the other option keeps popping up for you, this is your intuition gently letting you know that something is out of alignment. Sit quietly. Be still. Stop forcing a decision based on what makes sense logically and allow for your True Self to reveal how you really FEEL about it. Once you acknowledge what it is you REALLY want, what is ultimately best for you (I didn't say the actions that will have to come after your decision will be easy, though they might be, but they will be more true to what is MEANT for you to do), you will step into it 100% which will give you the freedom to move forward.

Day 12

Gratitude: Above all else, what are you grateful for?

Prompt: Whew! The past couple days have been spiritually freeing! Yes, you've done the digging – but let's celebrate the fact that you have stepped into the power of letting some STUFF go! You've released and finally made some decisions to move past where you have been stuck in turmoil. Today, we ask for guidance in the plan! We can't surrender our fears and then expect to execute the next steps by ourselves... that is stepping right back into force mode. Today I want you to start with the question: "What will You have me do today to best support my next steps?" Then, allow for the True You to throw creativity around like confetti and jot some of those ideas down!

Day 13

Gratitude: What makes you feel abundant?

Prompt: FUN. If you are like me, you have let the past couple days of digging, surrendering, trying hard not to judge yourself, releasing, and then co-creating a plan with the universe feel all heavy and serious. Today we focus on the FUN. What SOUNDS fun to you? What FEELS fun? What are some things you can do today that will allow for you to have fun on PURPOSE? When was the last time you seriously had a BLAST? Fun is the theme of the day... let your mind wander. Perhaps let the playful little child you once were come out through your words (I know it sounds corny, but umm, hi... as an adult, have you been able to match the excitement you felt about LIFE when you were a tiny human?). What will YOU do that is FUN today?

_____

_____

_____

_____

_____

_____

_____

_____

_____

_____

_____

Day 14

Gratitude: Shout it out... what feels fabulous?

Prompt: Are you willing to receive? When we go through the process of uncovering who we are, often we discover that we have put up blocks to receiving! We are fearful of asking for help. We are fearful of looking needy. We are fearful of appearing weak. But here's the thing... without the help, guidance, and support of others, we usually remain stuck. Today I encourage you to journal on how the concept of receiving makes you FEEL. Are you ready to bring in the people, money, experiences, gifts, words, lessons, situations, etc. that are going to aid you in impacting the world on the scale that you are meant to?

Gratitude: There is a lot going on and so much to be proud of... write it here!

Prompt: Yesterday we talked about being willing to receive, which I know for me was an interesting concept. We always focus on what we WANT but often set up our own blocks that keep those very things from us. Today, I'd love for you to sit quietly and allow that one THING that keeps weighing you down to come to the surface. When did you take on that limiting belief/ self-sabotaging thought/ worry?

Chances are, that fear that you are carrying is something you took on during a completely different season of your life and it just doesn't serve you anymore. (Example: still carrying fearful thoughts about how your body should look according to your high school self as opposed to recognizing the fact that life looks a lot different now than when you were in high school – you've had children, you've had surgeries, you've run marathons, etc.) I also would love for you to recognize how many times a day you THINK about this thought. What if you recognized that this thought no longer applies to where you are in life and you released yourself from thinking about it multiple times per day? Think about all the SPACE that would create, energetically, to allow for new, amazing things to come in.

Journal on this affirmation: "I release the baggage of _____ in order to free up space and be willing to receive what I truly want NOW."

_____

_____

_____

_____

_____

_____

Day 16

Gratitude: Cause goodness knows you are uncovering lots of good stuff!

Prompt: My favorite qualities in a human are_____. My favorite qualities in myself are_____. Do they match up? Does this matter to you?

_____

_____

_____

_____

_____

_____

_____

_____

_____

_____

_____

_____

_____

_____

_____

_____

Day 17

Gratitude: What makes your heart do a happy dance? (Sidebar story: I am well known in my family and friends circle for the "Jillie Dance". Picture simultaneously swinging your arms alternatively around in front of you, wiggling your hips, and shaking your head from side to side- hair flip and all. Whatever ridiculous picture you have in your head right now is probably completely on point and it is filled with JOY! Create your own personal dance and allow whatever you are grateful for to lead you to bust it out!)

Prompt: Having a "to-do" list for things that need to get done is great. Having an intentions-list for how you want to feel, unrelated to external circumstances, is the BEST. Set your intentions for the day, the week, the month, your life HERE! Starting small and working your way into big picture visions makes it not only excitingly doable, but also allows for you to find joy in the journey. Feel the feels first and then watch the things happen.

Day 18

Gratitude: What fills your cup?

Prompt: Who needs to feel your energy today? You are clearing space within you, stepping into who you truly are with joy, and letting go of what no longer serves you. You are basically a MAGNET for miracles and people are drawn to that energy. To whom can you share a smile, an uplifting comment, a cup of coffee, or a pat on the back today? Write a letter to someone who needs your internal sunshine here. Perhaps you give it to them for real, perhaps you read it to them, perhaps you simply write it and never tell them but trust that they FEEL your thoughts. Put goodness out there toward that one person and watch how your energy level recalibrates on an even higher level today!

Day 19

Gratitude: What are you grateful for? Doodle it out here!

Prompt: Free write! List everything you love. Just start listing them all out- people, memories, experiences, things, places, smells, feelings... list them out and become aware of them as they present themselves to you today. Know that you manifested them by taking the time to be present with your thoughts of them now!

_____

_____

_____

_____

_____

_____

_____

_____

_____

_____

_____

_____

_____

_____

Day 20

Gratitude: Oh to feel grateful, what a gift you give to yourself. Whether or not you have actually received the physical form of "the thing" yet, take the space below to honor this gift!

Prompt: Is there a piece of you that has been subdued for years and years? Is there a part of you that has been covered up, perhaps because other personality traits within you have been more boisterous and readily available to align with? Uncover that person. Uncover, see, and allow for that amazing person to come stand on the platform WITH the sides of you that have taken center stage all this time. You have not wrongly chosen to align with one side of you rather than another. You are not bad for keeping a piece of who you really are hidden. Release those fears. Recognize that it is your time to allow for ALL of you to intertwine and press forward as one – the whole you. Because you are all those things! All those versions of you within, even the one that has barely had a voice, make up the beauty and majesty of who you really are. Write about the parts of you that have been covered up and welcome that person into your whole self.

_____

_____

_____

_____

_____

_____

_____

_____

_____

Day 21

Gratitude: There is so much, but what makes you feel happy?

Prompt: "I want to thank you, thank you, thank you, thank you, thank you, thank you, thank you thank you..."- Natalie Merchant got it right in her song "Kind and Generous". We can spend all this time feeling the feels and acknowledging that we are grateful; but who/ what/ where would you like to extend a "Thank You"? Someone who has helped you along your path? A place that makes you feel at home? A cherished piece of jewelry? Say thank you to whomever or whatever you want in this space... Hint: Make sure to put yourself at the top of that list!

_____

_____

_____

_____

_____

_____

_____

_____

_____

_____

_____

Day 22

Gratitude: What are you grateful for, you superhuman of fabulousness?

Prompt: Trust the process. Answering all of these questions, writing all of these letters, letting your heart pour out onto the page and then feeling the aftermath of wonder or bewilderment can leave us wondering if it's worth it. It is. Reflect over the past three weeks; what have you noticed happening because you have been sticking with the process?

Day 23

Gratitude: Something feels amazing within you right now, what is it? Shout it out!

Prompt: How can you be helpful to someone else today? You have learned a lot over this new season of your life. Can you help others step into who they truly are by sharing with them something you have learned? Today, think about people in your life you can help or opportunities you have to change someone's life. Write about the opportune actions and how that would feel for you. Generate joy in helping someone before you even do it, then watch how beautifully everything falls into place as you take the action later on!

_____

_____

_____

_____

_____

_____

_____

_____

_____

_____

_____

_____

_____

Day 24

Gratitude: Give thanks to yourself for all that you have achieved... it sets the tone for your entire day. How can you best depict those things here?

Prompt: Ask yourself this question: How can I love myself more? What are some things you can do to show love to yourself? Are there conversations to be had? Are there places (physically or metaphorically) to be cleaned out to create space for more love? What do you presently need to feel more aligned with the feeling of love and how can you generate that for yourself?

_____
_____
_____
_____
_____
_____
_____
_____
_____
_____
_____
_____

Day 25

Gratitude: Let the feeling of gratitude swell within you!

Prompt: Abundance. Today, I encourage you to journal on your beliefs about abundance. According to Dictionary.com abundance means "an extremely plentiful or over sufficient quantity or supply". What does that word mean to YOU? What does abundance feel like? Do you believe your life to be abundant? Always? Sometimes? Never? Get good and honest with yourself here!

Day 26

Gratitude: List out the things that make you feel most alive!

Prompt: What sounds fun? You have gone through things in your life. You have goals and plans for the future. What is it, right now, that sounds completely ENJOYABLE and FUN!? When we make decisions by focusing on what "makes sense" or what "should be done", often we lose the connection to it because it's not all that fun anymore. Stop "shoulding" yourself and focus on "funning" yourself. Here is your opportunity today: the next time you have a decision to make, make it based solely on what sounds most FUN to you. Have fun on purpose!

_____

_____

_____

_____

_____

_____

_____

_____

_____

_____

_____

Day 27

Gratitude: Write it out and feel the words – what are you grateful for?

Prompt: Get rid of the word "JUST". You are not an inconvenience, you are not "simply" something... own your flipping greatness! Too often we downplay ourselves, our talents, our brilliance by saying, "Oh, I'm JUST me". No. Absolutely not. You ARE you. You are amazing. You are talented. You are creative. You are strong. And you are the only YOU that ever has been and ever will be. Where have you been playing small? Time to amplify it... you are not JUST anything!

_____

_____

_____

_____

_____

_____

_____

_____

_____

_____

_____

_____

_____

Day 28

Gratitude: What are you most significantly thankful for today? Draw, list words, doodle, enjoy!

Prompt: I want you to write about how this makes you feel: the same God (Universe, Creator, Source Energy, LOVE, etc.) that created each drop of water in the oceans, each tiny petal on every flower on the earth, each polar bear, bumble bee, owl... CARED enough to take the time to create YOU exactly as you are. Don't tell me that YOU don't matter. Don't tell me that YOU don't have a significant role to play. Don't tell me that YOU, the TRUE YOU, should stay bottled up inside because you are fearful of showing your brilliance.

Let that sink in... and then write. Feel the feels, let the tears flow, go there.

Day 29

Gratitude: What feels hot on your heart that just makes you ooze with beautiful gratitude?

Prompt: Change. What area of your life are you ready to make changes to because you finally know how it aligns with who you actually are? Relationships? Health? Finances? Business? Confidence? There is something brewing in there right now that you are feeling called to give your full attention to. Allow for yourself to get honest about how you can better maximize that area of your life. Get as specific as you want here. What area of your life do you want to make changes in and what are some things you can start doing immediately to do so?

_____

_____

_____

_____

_____

_____

_____

_____

_____

_____

_____

_____

Day 30

Gratitude: When we bring attention to that which we are thankful for, it amplifies! Keep the goodness coming!

Prompt: Fears and how to let go! Why are you scared? Remember that THING that you said yesterday you are ready to make changes to? What is it you were afraid of in the past that has kept you from making those changes? What are you scared of now as you step forward to actually do it? Are they the same thing? Today acknowledge the fear. See it, witness it for what it is, thank it for coming (maybe it kept you safe, maybe it served you for a time), let it know that it no longer matters, wish it well and release it. Write out everything that has made you afraid to make this change, surrender it up, and let it go.

_____

_____

_____

_____

_____

_____

_____

_____

_____

_____

_____

Day 31

Gratitude: What makes your whole being feel good?

Prompt: How can you better support yourself as you make the change you have been focusing on over the past two days? Do you need to meditate more to provide yourself an opportunity to receive guidance? Do you need to get rid of the junk food and download a guide on what "clean eating" means? Do you need to create a weekly exercise calendar that feels exciting and fun? Do you need to sit with your credit card statement and reflect upon where changes can be made? Do you need to hire a coach to ask you the tough questions and guide you to where you want to go? Do you need to make an exit strategy for leaving your soul-sucking job? Do you need to put "date night" on the calendar to guarantee alone time with your spouse? These are all very specific ideas on all sorts of topics that prove to you that you can take ACTION based on what FEELS GOOD. It's time to stop thinking you "should" do something (remember, no more "shoulding" yourself!) and step up to the plate with a supportive action that will allow for you to step forward. Write them down! This can be super fun and inspiring if you allow for it to be! You are providing yourself with the opportunity to receive help and create a plan!

Day 32

Gratitude: I know there is something amazing in there! What is it?

Prompt: Why? Why are you going to do this thing that you have been pushing to the side for so long? Why is this important? Why are you going to do it anyway – when things get hard, when you don't feel like it, when inspiration is long gone and you have to rely on personal integrity? Knowing why allows for you to honor yourself... let's get that reason down on paper.

_____

_____

_____

_____

_____

_____

_____

_____

_____

_____

_____

_____

_____

_____

Day 33

Gratitude: Oh there is so much to be grateful for... today those things are:

Prompt: It's time to write another letter. This time you are writing a letter from your Future Self to the you NOW. When you see your life through the eyes of the person you WILL be, you will have the desire to start doing what needs to be done now to get you there. How does your Future Self feel about the action you are taking now? What does "actually going for it now" look like for the you in the future? Congratulate yourself. Assuage any fears. Comfort yourself and remind yourself that, of course, it was worth it. Your future self is PROOF that it was all worth it. Give yourself reason why NOW from the vantage point of the you that has done it!

Day 34

Gratitude: What is it you are super thankful for?

Prompt: Forgiveness. We've already talked about the power of forgiveness in this journal, but it's a theme that you have the opportunity to revisit time and time again. Here's the thing. You are going to feel hurt. You are going to feel let down. You are going to feel like you aren't good enough. You are going to feel like you can't. But you also know that all these things are not truth. Today, especially now as you are energetically and logistically behind moving the needle forward in your life in at least one opportune area, forgive everyone and everything that has held you back. Let it go. Write it out. Speak to people specifically or speak to feelings generally... but make forgiveness the name of the game today and be free because of it!

Day 35

Gratitude: How beautiful this life is and I am so grateful for...

Prompt: Freedom is...

_____

_____

_____

_____

_____

_____

_____

_____

_____

_____

_____

_____

_____

_____

_____

Day 36

Gratitude: Name the people, things, feelings, places you love so much!

Prompt: Finish this sentence, "Hi my name is _____ and I _____". Take this wherever you would like to go. My sense is, at this point, you have a far deeper understanding of who you are, what you do, what brings you joy, what you are willing to receive in your life, and where you are going. It's AMAZING to have those feelings... but, in order for you to step into your new truth (or rather, the truth that has been there all along but you have just recently given yourself the grace of uncovering) you need to SAY IT. You need to OWN IT. You need to declare "THIS is who I am... THIS is what I love... THIS is what I am creating... THIS is what I am meant for." Hint: as you grow as your True Self forever and ever you will have the opportunity to constantly pivot, tweak, and re-declare this sentiment! How exciting! So write it out! Who ARE you? Oooooh this is fun!

_____

_____

_____

_____

_____

_____

_____

_____

_____

_____

Day 37

Gratitude: What makes your heart sing?

Prompt: Ask for what you need. We've done this once before and we are doing it again. We spend so much time walking around thinking about what we want or need to get done, worrying how we are going to get it done, and allowing for the stress to pile up because when it is within us it seems so daunting. However, when it comes down to it, we don't ASK for the support we need. Today, what do you need? Where do you need support? Where can you surrender and let God (LOVE) take over? Where can you ask a spouse, friend, or colleague for support in an area that has been bogging you down? Get specific and ask for help! Take it off your plate, out of your mind, and out of your energetic space by DOING rather than, only THINKING about it.

Day 38

Gratitude: Today I am thankful for _____!

Prompt: Where are you stronger now than you were before? What areas of your life do you feel better in because you have given yourself the gift of journaling?

_____
_____
_____
_____
_____
_____
_____
_____
_____
_____
_____
_____
_____
_____
_____
_____

Gratitude: Reflection is not only what physically looks back at you from a mirror, but it is remembering and being impacted by your past self. Why does your past make you feel grateful?

Prompt: Reflection opportunity... have people noticed anything different in you? What compliments have you been given? Do you feel lighter when you walk into the room? Write all these things out! As we transform, it is important that we take note of the acknowledgement we receive! It's nice to be noticed! We must first notice ourselves and then we must notice other people noticing us! What a tribute to that person, when we acknowledge the fact that they noticed something within us!

Day 40

Gratitude: What makes you smile?

Prompt: What advice would you give to someone who needs it? There is someone NOW struggling with something that you were struggling with in the past... write out what you would say to that person. (Hint: this reaffirms for you just how far you have come!)

_____
_____
_____
_____
_____
_____
_____
_____
_____
_____
_____
_____
_____
_____
_____
_____

Day 41

Gratitude: The universe wants to know, what gifts of love have you received that you are so thankful for?

Prompt: Blocks. What is blocking you from stepping into brilliance in a certain area? You have released many, but have you noticed any new blocks popping up for you as you have progressed through your self-discovery process? Write them out and don't allow for them to control you! You are in charge!

Day 42

Gratitude: It is important to be grateful for roadblocks. Sometimes they help point you in a new direction, a detour that must be taken in order to get to your true destination. What roadblocks are you grateful for?

Prompt: Get out of the funk! As we start to uncover who we are, what brings us joy, and where we truly intend to go with this life we tap into a feeling of FLOW... and it feels good. But what about those times that your energy is just off and you just feel funky? If you are like me, you start to get all heady and try to force yourself out of that state of blah and back into the flow. You try to control good feelings and "snap yourself out of it". You use the phrase, "I just have to figure this out". My friend. Stop. Take a deep, rejuvenating, forgiving breath. Feel the feels. It's okay if you slipped a little out of a flowy state, because you will get back there... but you will only get back there through natural actions of love and trust. Journal on this today. What can you do LESS OF in order to gain MORE peace and flow?

_____

_____

_____

_____

_____

_____

_____

_____

_____

Day 43

Gratitude: Keep it simple today – why are you thankful?

Prompt: Repeat this affirmation: "I am worthy and I intentionally choose a life that flows with joy, love, wealth, support, and empowerment." Feel that affirmation in your heart and let the words fill the pages!

_____

_____

_____

_____

_____

_____

_____

_____

_____

_____

_____

_____

_____

_____

_____

Day 44

Gratitude: There are so many things, but the first things that come to my mind are...

Prompt: The big dreams I have for my life are _____. I am creating them by _____. Right now you ARE creating the life of your dreams. So, talk about it and give yourself credit. You showing up now, has everything to do with what you will have/ be/ feel in the future. Make a list and write it out.

_____

_____

_____

_____

_____

_____

_____

_____

_____

_____

_____

_____

_____

_____

Day 45

Gratitude: What is in your heart today that is bursting to come out?

Prompt: Yesterday we celebrated the fact that everything we are doing now is creating what we intend to have/ be/ feel in the future. What a miracle, right?! But let's not forget, that everything we did in the past has brought us to the here and now! What you have now was once a goal or dream of your Past Self. Start your journaling today by saying "thank you" to your Past Self for having the dreams, wisdom, insight, and tenacity to bring you here – to the life you are living right now. What a gift!

_____

_____

_____

_____

_____

_____

_____

_____

_____

_____

_____

_____

Day 46

Gratitude: What matters to you most? Why are you grateful for those things?

Prompt: Today I encourage you to start your journaling off with the phrase, "I matter" and follow those words up with whatever comes forth! (Hint: Did you add "me" to what matters most to you?)

_____
_____
_____
_____
_____
_____
_____
_____
_____
_____
_____
_____
_____
_____
_____
_____

Day 47

Gratitude: Goodness, there is so much to be grateful for and today those things include...

Prompt: Today I would like for you to lovingly remember what you USED to (do, think, believe, say, etc.) and admiringly follow that statement up with what you CHOOSE to (do, think, believe, say, etc.) now. We are looking to recognize growth in this journal entry. We are not here to judge your Past Self... why would you do that? You have learned so much from that person! We want to acknowledge all that we have progressed through that has led us to now! (Hint: this might be a cool time to bring up your FEARS and TRUTHS columns that you made at the beginning of this journey. Is it time to make a new one? I won't add lines to this space so you can create two new columns if you would like to!)

Day 48

Gratitude! Today I am so thankful for...

Prompt: Today I feel_____.

_____

_____

_____

_____

_____

_____

_____

_____

_____

_____

_____

_____

_____

_____

_____

_____

_____

Day 49

Gratitude: I am unbelievably grateful for _____ qualities that I possess.

Prompt: How will you show up as your BEST self today? Who can you serve? How will you emanate abundance? What will you teach? Where will you go? Allow for your intuition and your joy to guide you!

_____

_____

_____

_____

_____

_____

_____

_____

_____

_____

_____

_____

_____

_____

_____

_____

_____

Day 50

Gratitude: I am grateful today, and always for...

Prompt: As we conclude this season of your journaling experience, this Self-Discovery time period, this moment of letting the TRUE YOU shine through... what do you BELIEVE? What do you know to be true? What are you steadfast in your belief of?

And of course, let's finish this the way we started: WHO ARE YOU!?

Trust yourself... go there. Let it out!

_____

_____

_____

_____

_____

_____

_____

_____

_____

_____

_____

_____

Conclusion

It's funny to type the word "conclusion" here because really, you've just begun- and thank goodness for that! But it is super important to note that every new chapter does come to an end to allow the next chapter to begin! Our lives, our majesty, our presence is a constant story book that transitions from one page to the next, one chapter to the next. There is no concluding cover because everything we do in life has energetic ripple effects that will progress forward and emanate into the world for the rest of time.

Through this process of learning a new skill to deepen your level of self-discovery, you have simply enhanced the opportunity you have to show up in this abundant universe.

I hope the daily focus on gratitude served your heart. I hope the prompts allowed for you to uncover hidden gems that had previously been laying dormant in you, yearning to be discovered. I hope you were able to feel the power of releasing what no longer serves you. I pray that you were able to feel the power of stepping into the brilliance that you were intuitively being called to step into.

Know that you can (and should) return to this journal whenever you feel called to it. Perhaps going through the entire 50 days will become an annual tradition. Perhaps you felt super connected to a few of the prompts and will focus on those and integrate those into your daily journaling practice. Perhaps you will pick a prompt that you and a partner, friend, spouse, etc. can work through together. Perhaps a friend in need will come to you for help and you can serve them with a prompt that you feel will benefit them. Whatever it is… use the gifts that you have given yourself through this experience to guide you in whatever capacity you feel called to forever and ever.

Never forget that the True You that is within is brilliant, strong, and worthy. Journaling is an incredibly powerful portal through which that light can brightly shine. And when you shine your true light bright and proud, those that are blessed to being in your presence will feel the warmth of the glow and in turn will feel inspired to tap into their True Light.

Shine brightly friends. Let your abundant sunshine glow!

With empowering love,

Jillian

P.S. I LOVE hearing from the empowered hearts who feel connected to the love I enjoy pouring into the world. For further help and guidance – or just to say hello – please find me at www.jillianbolanz.com or send me an email at *jillian@jillianbolanz.com*.

Also, I love social media so come give me a virtual hug on iTunes and subscribe to my podcast "Morning Sunshine with Jillian Bolanz", Instagram @jillianbolanz (I LOVE IG Stories!) or Facebook www.facebook.com/JillianBolanz . This amazing world is filled with abundant opportunities to connect and make an impact on one another! Let's use them to spread joy, light, and love!

About the Author

Jillian Bolanz is a mamapreneur who loves the harmony that is ever flowing between her True Self's work as a Life Coach/Business Strategist/Online Fitness and Wellness Mentor and her dream of being home and present with her two sons.

Up until a few years ago, she lived her whole life according to what SHE SHOULD do as opposed to what SHE WANTED to do. And when she finally let her heart lead the way, everything changed. Through journaling, personal development, getting curious about her passions, and leaning into trust, she has stepped into who she really is as a guide, a connector, and a forever learner and teacher.

Jillian's followers are constantly inspired by her Live Broadcasts on social media platforms like Facebook (www.facebook.com/JillianBolanz) and Instagram (@jillianbolanz). She also LOVES giving 5 minute morning powerhouse pep talks as well as conducting empowering interviews on her podcast "Morning Sunshine with Jillian Bolanz". Her inspiration, positivity, real talk, and ability to love people through the process of their own self-discovery feels like sunshine as it pours from her heart into those she gets to serve in this capacity, through one-to-one Life Coaching, and in her Transformational Group Mastermind.

Jillian is obsessed with giving women the tools to energetically and logistically create a life of confidence, empowerment, and self-belief. She loves helping these impassioned souls make the impact (& income) that they were MEANT to make.

Jillian lives in the beautiful state of Maine with her husband and love of her life, Michael, and their two sons, Cameron and Andrew. She loves exercise, wine, and connecting deeply with whomever she speaks!

For more information on opportunities to work with Jillian, please visit **www.jillianbolanz.com/contact**

Made in the USA
Lexington, KY
29 November 2017